# Eckley Miners' Village

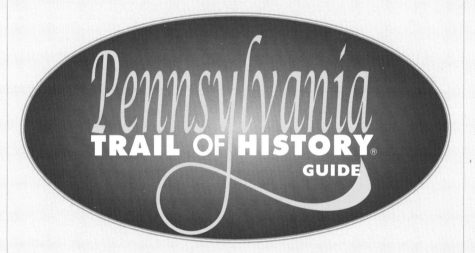

*Pennsylvania*
**TRAIL OF HISTORY**®
**GUIDE**

*Text by Perry Blatz*
*Photographs by Craig A. Benner*

## STACKPOLE BOOKS

PENNSYLVANIA HISTORICAL
AND MUSEUM COMMISSION

Kyle R. Weaver, Series Editor
Tracy Patterson, Designer

Published by
STACKPOLE BOOKS
5067 Ritter Road
Mechanicsburg, Pennsylvania 17055

Pennsylvania Trail of History® is a registered trademark of the Pennsylvania Historical and Museum Commission.

Printed in the United States of America
2   4   6   8   10   9   7   5   3   1
FIRST EDITION

Maps by Caroline Stover

Photography
Craig A. Benner: cover, 3, 5, 12, 33, 35–47

**Library of Congress Cataloging-in-Publication Data**

Blatz, Perry K.
    Eckley Miners' Village : Pennsylvania trail of history guide / text by Perry Blatz ; photographs by Craig A. Benner.—1st ed.
        p.   cm.—(Pennsylvania trail of history guides)
    Includes bibliographical references.
    ISBN 0-8117-2741-6
    1. Eckley Miners' Village (Eckley, Pa.)—Guidebooks. 2. Eckley (Pa.)—Guidebooks. 3. Eckley Miners' Village (Eckley, Pa.)—History. 4. Eckley (Pa.)—History. 5. Mining camps—Pennsylvania—Eckley—History. 6. Coal miners—Pennsylvania—Eckley—History. 7. Coal mines and mining—Pennsylvania—Eckley—History. I. Benner, Craig A. II. Pennsylvania Historical and Museum Commission. III. Title. IV. Series.

F159.E174 B57 2003
974.8'32—dc21

                                                                                    2002014133

# Contents

# Editor's Preface

Pennsylvania history is deeply rooted in its anthracite heritage. So significant is the legacy of anthracite that the Pennsylvania Historical and Museum Commission (PHMC) has created an entire complex of museums in northeastern Pennsylvania to commemorate the industry. With this new volume of the Pennsylvania Trail of History Guides, Stackpole Books is pleased to showcase Eckley Miners' Village, a site that preserves an anthracite company town that was once a part of the Council Ridge Colliery.

Each volume of the Pennsylvania Trail of History Guides focuses on a historic site or museum administered by the PHMC. The series was conceived and created by Stackpole Books with the cooperation of the PHMC's Division of Publications and Bureau of Historic Sites and Museums. Donna Williams heads the latter, and she and her staff of professionals review the text of each guidebook for accuracy and have made many valuable recommendations. Diane Reed, Chief of Publications, has facilitated relations between the PHMC and Stackpole from the project's inception, organized the review process with the commission, and attended to numerous details related to the venture.

David Dubick, Administrator of Eckley Miners' Village, was a spirited guide whose valuable insights on Eckley and its people contributed significantly to this volume. Chester Kulesa, Curator at the Anthracite Heritage Museum, worked diligently in the archives of both sites to furnish the historic images that document life at Eckley. Craig A. Benner has once again used his expert eye and camera to produce magnificent photographs of the site today.

Perry Blatz, the author of the text, is Associate Professor of History at Duquesne University in Pittsburgh and author of *Democratic Miners: Work and Labor Relations in the Anthracite Coal Industry, 1875–1925*. Dedicating his efforts on this volume to his wife Kathleen, he gives a brief overview of the anthracite industry in Pennsylvania, then fully delineates the rise of Council Ridge, the work at the colliery, the community life of the workers and their families at Eckley, labor struggles, and the eventual decline of anthracite in the twentieth century. He completes the guide with an armchair tour of the village as it is preserved today.

Kyle R. Weaver, Editor
Stackpole Books

# Introduction to the Site

Eckley Miners' Village was a town built around a coal mine that opened in 1854. The company that operated the mine established the town at the same time so mine workers would have a place to live in this rather remote part of Pennsylvania. The village is in the middle of the anthracite coal region, extending through the east-central and northeastern parts of the state, where hard coal was mined in large quantities from the 1820s through the 1960s. Thousands of immigrants lived and worked in this company town, as they did in similar communities throughout the state to mine coal and do other industrial work that made Pennsylvania the nation's "Titan of Industry."

Administered today by the Pennsylvania Historical and Museum Commission, the site includes eleven original nineteenth-century buildings, two structures reconstructed from their original nineteenth-century plans, one nineteenth-century church moved to the site, one mid-twentieth-century building, a visitor center, and three buildings constructed as props in 1968 during the filming of a movie in Eckley. A number of other original houses in the town are still privately occupied. Eckley Miners' Village has hosted numerous exhibits, conferences, cultural events, and educational programs since it opened to the public in 1975. Its many activities are supported by the Eckley Miners' Village Associates, a volunteer organization. The site is one of several state historic sites interpreting the history of the anthracite coal region. The others are the Museum of Anthracite Mining in Ashland, the Pennsylvania Anthracite Heritage Museum in Scranton, and the Scranton Iron Furnaces.

# Industrial Genesis

E ckley Miners' Village is a quiet, almost quaint place today. But for about a century, beginning some 150 years ago, it exemplified the clamor and conflict of the anthracite coal industry, which almost singlehandedly fueled the early stages of America's industrial revolution. Like many other communities founded in Pennsylvania in the nineteenth century, it was a company town. Because the coal was here, the men who established Eckley had no choice but to build a town too. Such employers took on a far larger set of responsibilities—providing workers and their families with necessities such as housing and medical care and basic amenities like a store, a school, and churches. They took this unusual role in their workers' lives, not out of kindness, but to attract workers to do the difficult work of mining in this remote place. Along with many other little coal towns in Pennsylvania, it was called a "coal patch," for its singular purpose and rural surroundings. Nevertheless, the village of Eckley attracted immigrants from many nations of Europe from the mid-nineteenth century into the twentieth. To earn a steady income, they would put up with the hardships and control that

came with life in a company town. But over the years, they would find a great many ways to make that town their own.

The story of this place and the people who lived and worked here is one of dynamic economic and social change, but its most recent chapter tells us why Eckley, like many places in America's Northeast and Midwest, is so quiet today. Coal, America's first industrial fuel in the nineteenth century, was pushed aside by petroleum and its by-products as the twentieth century progressed. As the demand for coal languished, the pace of life at Eckley slowed. Most of its residents were forced to leave for whatever new opportunities they could find, just as millions of mine workers and their families did over the years across the nation.

## THE ANTHRACITE INDUSTRY

For much of the nineteenth and early twentieth centuries, anthracite, or hard coal, served as the major home-heating fuel for the northeastern and midwestern United States, as well as an important industrial fuel. During the heyday of the anthracite industry, from the 1870s to the 1920s, from 100,000 to 180,000 mine workers labored in and around several hundred coal mines. Practically

*Eckley Breaker, c. 1901.* ECKLEY MINERS' VILLAGE

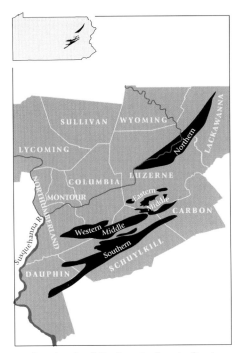

***Anthracite Coal Basins.*** *Anthracite lies in four basins in northeastern Pennsylvania.*

all of the nation's commercially viable anthracite could be found in 484 square miles of coal land across nine counties in east-central and northeastern Pennsylvania. Their location is best visualized today in reference to the main highway from Harrisburg to Scranton, I-81, built after most of the mines had closed. The westernmost deposits of anthracite are located about twenty-five miles northeast of Harrisburg. Mines could be found on either side of what would become I-81, almost all of them within about fifteen miles. The swaths of coal land stretched to the northeast past Pottsville and Wilkes-Barre to Scranton, as the highway does today, with the northeastern edge of coal deposits extending farther to end about twenty miles northeast of Scranton. The coal lands were grouped into four separate fields, the largest of which were the northern, or Wyoming, field, mainly in Lackawanna and north-

ern Luzerne Counties, and the southern, or Schuylkill, field, mainly in Schuylkill County. In between were the western-middle and eastern-middle, or Lehigh, fields. Eckley Miners' Village is located in the eastern-middle field, in southern Luzerne County.

Driving along I-81, today's traveler cannot help but notice the massive and rugged wooded ridges extending to the horizon. These made this part of William Penn's colony a wild and forbidding place when European settlers first began to look toward it in the middle of the eighteenth century. At that time, England experienced the first stirrings of the industrial revolution, fueled by ample supplies of coal. So early settlers of northeastern Pennsylvania had more than an inkling of the potential power and wealth that coal could provide as they began to find it in outcrops, visible along hills and cliffs. But what would eventually be seen as the great virtue of anthracite coal initially limited its use. Anthracite burns cleaner than any other coal, but it is far more difficult than the softer, bituminous variety to ignite and keep burning, so much so that it acquired the nickname of "stone coal." The first successful use of anthracite recorded was in 1769 by Obadiah Gore, a Wilkes-Barre blacksmith. Anthracite's first industrial use occurred in 1788, again in Wilkes-Barre, when Judge Jesse Fell used it to manufacture nails. To make anthracite a successful home-heating fuel, however, someone had to find a way to keep it burning on its own, without blowing air through it. The crucial step was to burn anthracite in an open grate. While several individuals claimed to have done so before Judge Fell did in 1808, he publicized his success sufficiently to heighten awareness of what would eventually become anthracite's most important use.

The decades in which anthracite was found in northeastern Pennsylvania and gradually recognized as a potentially valuable fuel coincided with the founding of the United States and the purchase by the Coxe family of the land that would become Eckley Miners' Village. The Coxes showed interest in American land at about the same time as William Penn. An English physician named Daniel Coxe turned his energies toward buying land in what would become New Jersey. He was even appointed governor of the colony of West Jersey, although he never crossed the Atlantic. But his son did so, and his grandson William Coxe established himself as a successful merchant in Philadelphia. One of William's thirteen children was Tench Coxe, who would purchase the coal lands that would lead his descendants out of the financial struggles that dominated his own life. Tench, born in 1755, began work with his father's mercantile business in 1775, the year before the United States declared its independence. Like many members of his family, he remained loyal to the British in the early years of the American Revolution, first following them to New York, and then returning with them to Philadelphia when they held that city in the winter of 1777–78. Once the British abandoned Philadelphia, Tench cast his lot with the rebels, although he had to fend off charges of disloyalty for the rest of his life.

After the end of the American Revolution, Tench Coxe became more and more involved in land acquisition and speculation, purchasing sizable tracts of land in northeastern Pennsylvania beginning in the 1780s, including the land that is now Eckley Miners' Village. Meanwhile, he was one of a growing chorus of entrepreneurial citizens to call for a new constitution to strengthen the fledgling nation. Coxe served as an official in the Washington administration and helped Secretary of the Treasury Alexander Hamilton draft his *Report on Manufactures*, which began to open the eyes of Americans to the nation's industrial potential. A contentious figure, Coxe served in a number of national and state administrations in succeeding decades until shortly before his death in 1824. He never experienced the success he thought he deserved, and struggled to pay debts from his continual land speculation, an economic activity that had the dynamic possibilities and pitfalls today's Americans find in the stock market. But the one constant in the lengthy and controversial career of Tench Coxe was his tireless promotion of and confidence in American economic and industrial growth.

The entrepreneurial vigor of the new nation can be seen in the men who staked their future on the unlikely prospect that they could indeed make money by mining anthracite coal and getting it to market. The first efforts to mine anthracite commercially occurred in 1792, on Summit Hill some eighty miles northwest of Philadelphia near the Lehigh River. When a hunter named Philip Ginter found coal there, he informed Col. Jacob Weiss, a prominent local citizen who had been deputy quartermaster for the Revolutionary Army. After trading some land with Ginter, Colonel Weiss organized the Lehigh Coal Mining Company, including among its investors Robert Morris, financier of the American Revolution and signer of the Declaration of Independence. But the little coal mined at that time proved difficult to market, even to local blacksmiths. Initial efforts to transport coal down the rapids-strewn Lehigh proved disastrous. The company struggled, with its most notable achievement being the shipment of six wooden barges of coal to Philadelphia. The company sold the coal to the city to provide steam for a pump at the waterworks, but the plant's operators could not get the coal to burn.

## ESTABLISHING A MARKET FOR ANTHRACITE

The anthracite industry would have little future until it could shape its market. The nation's two largest cities, New York and Philadelphia, had both begun to use coal from Virginia and even from England as an alternative to wood, more and more difficult to obtain cheaply as the cities grew. When the War of 1812 disrupted American shipping and access to that coal, Jacob Cist, Colonel Weiss's nephew and the son of one of his partners, saw an opportunity. Having inherited his father's stock in the dormant Lehigh Coal Mining Company, he found some new partners and reactivated mining at Summit Hill in 1813. He then set out to prove to Philadelphians that not only could anthracite be burned, but it also was a superior fuel. He designed stoves to burn anthracite effectively for home heating, encouraged numerous craftsmen to try it for various industrial uses, and publicized those successes in newspaper articles and testimonials.

Although Cist took vital steps in both mining Lehigh coal and establishing a market for it, one of his customers, Josiah White, went much farther. After some initial struggles, White and his partner, Erskine Hazard, found anthracite the ideal fuel for their nail and wire mill on the Schuylkill River in the Manayunk section of Philadelphia. As entrepreneurs like Andrew Carnegie and John D. Rockefeller would do with such success some fifty years later, White expanded his business through the process known as vertical integration, taking on a range of business activities, from the production of raw materials through the transport

and sale of the finished product. He took control of Cist's mine in 1818 and moved to improve its nine-mile road to the Lehigh River as well as navigation on the river itself. Despite years on the edge of bankruptcy struggling to find enough capital, White incorporated the Lehigh Coal and Navigation Company in 1824. That year, the company shipped more than nine thousand tons of coal through its own recently constructed town on the Lehigh, Mauch Chunk, known today as Jim Thorpe.

Similar struggles toward economic development took place throughout the Middle Atlantic states and New England in the 1820s, 1830s, and 1840s to provide the foundation for America's industrial revolution. These decades began with a mania for canal building, ignited by the completion in 1825 of the Erie Canal, on which boats laden with people and freight could travel at the magnificent speed of about four miles per hour. Meanwhile, during the 1820s, the indefatigable Josiah White looked for ways to get his increasingly large shipments of anthracite to Philadelphia more quickly. He first presided over the construction of dams on the Lehigh from Mauch Chunk (now Jim Thorpe) to Easton to improve navigation. But from 1827 to 1829, his Lehigh Coal and Navigation Company constructed a far more reliable, thirty-six-mile-long towpath canal.

The increased pace of economic activity along the Lehigh River mirrored similar efforts around Wilkes-Barre and Carbondale to the north and Pottsville to the west. Throughout the anthracite fields in these decades, entrepreneurs like White opened mines, hired workers, improved transportation, and promoted the use of the fuel. Shipments of anthracite skyrocketed, from the first annual recording of 365 tons in 1820

***Transporting Anthracite.*** *Canals and railroads provided efficient means for hauling anthracite from mine to market, causing a boom in the anthracite industry.* ANTHRACITE HERITAGE MUSEUM

to 175,000 tons in 1830, 865,000 in 1840, and more than 3.3 million tons by 1850, largely as a result of rapidly declining transportation costs. Cheaper anthracite made it easier for the expanding ranks of craftsmen and entrepreneurs to discover that hard coal was a fine heat source for manufacturing processes like baking, sugar refining, distilling and brewing, making ceramics and chemicals, and, after a number of false starts, transforming iron ore into iron. Similarly, anthracite proved itself an excellent fuel for providing steam to power the growing numbers of ever more sophisticated machines. With steam power, manufacturing would no longer be restricted to those places that dominated America's earliest industrial efforts, where falling water could drive water wheels.

## GROWTH SPURRED BY ANTHRACITE
The result was not only rapid urban growth for cities like Philadelphia and New York, but even faster growth for small cities in and around the anthracite region like Mauch Chunk, Pottsville, Wilkes-Barre, Scranton, Allentown, Easton, Trenton, and Newark. To spur this

dynamic development, a new form of transportation was needed to go where canals couldn't. By the end of the 1820s, railroads arose to extend the reach of the canals. From the 1840s, rails were filling in the map of the northeastern United States, connecting mines, mills, factories, and cities, vastly strengthening the magnetic power of American economic growth to attract hundreds of thousands of immigrants, especially those fleeing agricultural poverty in Ireland and Germany.

All of this growth demanded coal, and in the Lehigh anthracite region, groups of investors laboriously assembled the capital to extend the railroad network northward from Mauch Chunk along the Lehigh River, then westward to new coal lands. In the 1830s and 1840s, mines opened in the Beaver Meadow and Hazleton coal basins, just a few miles south of the Big Black Creek coal basin. In 1854, anticipating the completion of the Jeddo and Carbon County Railroad, a group of local entrepreneurs decided that the time had come to make a deal with the Coxe family to open a mine on the long-dormant land they owned there.

# History of Eckley Miners' Village

The leading partners of the firm who founded the village of Eckley and the Council Ridge colliery (the mine and its associated buildings) were Asa Lansford Foster, John Leisenring, Richard Sharpe, and Francis Weiss. All were veterans of the coal industry with ties to Josiah White's Lehigh Coal and Navigation Company (LCNC) and its town of Mauch Chunk. These men differed greatly from the absentee stockholders and distant corporate managers who would increasingly control American business as the nineteenth century proceeded. They all spent most of their time living at and actively managing the mine, as did most of the other independent operators who dominated the early decades of the anthracite coal industry.

The oldest of the leading partners was Asa Lansford Foster, for whom the township in which Eckley is located was named. Born in Massachusetts in 1799, he married the niece of an engineer for the LCNC. He came to Mauch Chunk to operate the company's store there in 1826, and when the company later closed it, he opened his own store. He thought that substantial coal deposits could be found north of Summit Hill under Buck Mountain at the eastern edge of the Black Creek basin. In 1836, once the Lehigh Canal had been extended to the north, he established the Buck Mountain Coal Company just a few miles from what would eventually become Eckley. His mining operations succeeded for the next few years, but Foster had to sell his business at a loss when a flood damaged the northern portion of the canal. In 1844, he returned to Mauch Chunk, where he went to work for a mining contractor named Daniel Bertsch, the father-in-law of John Leisenring.

John Leisenring would serve as the linchpin connecting the leading partners. Born in 1819, his family came to Mauch Chunk before he turned ten. His father ran the LCNC's hotel and later found work for him on the company's engineering corps. Leisenring worked on a number of railroad and canal projects until 1844, when he married Caroline Bertsch. Shortly thereafter, he went to work with his father-in-law, contracting for the LCNC.

Richard Sharpe was born in England in 1813 and came to America at age thirteen with his father. He moved to Summit Hill in 1840 to work on projects for the LCNC, and in 1845 he went to work with Daniel Bertsch and John Leisenring.

The last of the leading partners to join the group, Francis Weiss, had the

*Miner's Double Dwelling at Eckley Miners' Village.*

deepest roots in the anthracite industry. Six months younger than Leisenring, he was the grandson of Col. Jacob Weiss, who had assembled the earliest organized mining effort in the anthracite region. After performing a variety of surveying work on local canals and railroads from the time he was eighteen, he joined with Leisenring in contract work for the LCNC in 1845. When the partners made the lease with the Coxes and went to work on opening the mine at Council Ridge, they all lived in the new village they built around it—Leisenring until 1859, Foster until his death in 1869, Weiss until 1870, and Sharpe until 1874. Some combination of these men and their relatives operated the mine and surrounding village until 1886.

The partners moved quickly to construct the mine and adjacent company town. When the mine made its first coal shipments in 1855, there were some 80 houses for about five hundred residents. By 1858, the number of houses had grown to 127 for some nine hundred residents. By 1860, the population exceeded one thousand, about one-quarter of them workers employed in and around the Council Ridge mine. The village was laid out along Main Street, which ran east-west for a little less than a mile. Within a few hundred yards of the center of town off Main Street were the breaker and mine entrance. The houses, of wooden-plank construction, were arrayed close together, with long lots extending away from the street on either side for about two hundred feet. The major village buildings were to the west, along with several big houses owned by resident partners, a number of the larger, two-and-a-half-story double houses, and Episcopal and Presbyterian churches. To the east, separated by a creek that ran by the breaker, were a greater number of smaller, one-and-a-half-story double houses arrayed along Main Street, with a Roman Catholic church and its rectory, completed late in 1861, at the far end.

This layout reflected a kind of residential segregation, in which the mine operators, their relatives, supervisors, and skilled craftsmen, all of whom were likely to be Protestant and, if not born in America, from England or Wales, lived in the bigger homes in the west end of town. The rest of the workforce, likely to be Irish Catholics, generally lived on the east end. Throughout industrializing America in this era, the longer someone had been in America and the greater his

*The Founders of Council Ridge and the Village of Eckley. From left to right, Asa Lansford Foster, John Leisenring, Richard Sharpe, and Francis Weiss.* ECKLEY MINERS' VILLAGE

# FOUNDING A COMPANY TOWN

Eckley was a company town or "coal patch," like a great many others in the rapidly developing anthracite region. Those terms convey an image of rigidly controlled life, both at work and at the homes surrounding the mine, where the managers of the mine and town exploited a captive population of mine workers. This image of a company town contains a good deal of truth in many places at many times. The company town was not organized for that purpose, however, but for a far more basic one. Coal entrepreneurs had to construct buildings adjacent to the mines to clean and process the coal, such as the massive coal breakers, a few of which still dot northeastern Pennsylvania. Because workers in those days could not commute to work, mine operators also had to provide housing around the mine for their employees, as well as basic amenities, such as a store, doctor's office, hotel, schools, and churches, some of which remain today as the most prominent buildings in Eckley Miners' Village.

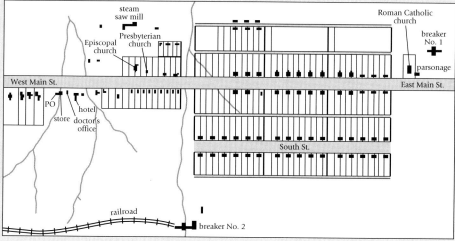

*Plan of the Village of Eckley.*

skill and experience, either in America or overseas, the higher status and larger income he and his family were likely to have. Irish and Germans dominated immigration to America in the 1840s, after a great many Welsh and English had already arrived, and before even larger numbers of Eastern and Southern Europeans began coming in the 1880s. Analysis of Eckley's population in the census of 1860 by historian Mary Ann Landis shows that more than half of Eckley's workers were Irish, most of them in low-paid laborers' positions. But even in Eckley's early days, Irish immigrants made better opportunities for themselves, with two listed as high-ranking supervisors just six years after the mine opened. Just as important, a company town like Eckley was a very small place, where the focus on mining and the lack of alternative activities tended to keep people from getting as far apart as they might have wanted. Thus, outside of work, the poorest laborer would encounter his bosses and even the leading partners and their families from time to time.

## WORK AND WORKERS
Production grew quickly at Council Ridge, exceeding one hundred thousand tons in 1857. The workforce in these

*Breaker Boys.* The youngest and most numerous aboveground workers at the colliery sat over the chutes in the breaker picking slate from the coal. ANTHRACITE HERITAGE MUSEUM

years was approximately 275, but in this mine, as throughout the anthracite industry, less than half of these men actually mined and loaded coal. About one-third of the workers were employed aboveground, performing such work as operating engines to provide power, removing impurities from the coal in the breaker, sorting it into useful sizes for the market, loading it into railroad cars, and dumping the accumulated refuse. The most numerous aboveground workers were the youngest, the breaker boys or slate pickers, most of whom were preteens, some as young as seven or eight. Working ten-hour days, they spent most of their time hunched over chutes along which various sizes of coal flowed, grabbing pieces of dirt and slate. Older men also worked in the breaker, once they were judged too old to labor underground.

After this introduction to the anthracite industry, most boys went underground, where about two-thirds of the workforce was employed. The boys usually started down below by opening ventilation doors. They spent long hours trying to stay alert enough to hear a bell attached to a load of cars for which they had to open their doors. In their teens, boys moved on to become mule drivers, transporting coal cars. Other underground workers included carpenters, men and boys preparing coal cars to be hoisted to the surface, and bosses to monitor the progress and safety of the work.

The remainder of the workers—the miners and laborers—did the basic work of mining. At Council Ridge, slopes from the surface took diagonal paths to

*Boys Underground* operated ventilation doors and drove mules that hauled the coal from the mine. ANTHRACITE HERITAGE MUSEUM

the coal veins, and the major passage-ways, known as gangways, were dug through the coal once the slope reached a vein. From the gangways, miners blasted out coal in numerous rooms, also called chambers or breasts, from twenty-four to thirty-six feet wide that could proceed through the vein as far as two hundred yards. Pillars of coal of about the same width were left between the rooms to support the surface. The miner focused on setting a pattern of black-powder charges deep enough into the face of the coal to extract the maxi-mum amount without blasting the coal into dust. He also had the responsibility, specified in state law from the 1870s, to keep his mining chamber safe, especially from the most common cause of acci-dents, roof falls. To do so, he set up wooden props as needed. While prac-tices varied from mine to mine and from one part of the anthracite region to another, a miner usually shared his tasks with a partner or worked with a laborer.

One thing that separated mine work-ers from factory workers was their greater independence, with the miner experienc-ing little daily supervision. Generally the miner worked as a relatively independent contractor, receiving a certain sum for each car of coal. From his earnings, the miner had to buy his powder, fuses, tools, and fuel for his lamp, and also pay his laborer a portion of what he received per car. In addition to extracting coal from a chamber, the most-skilled miners submit-ted bids on specific contracts for special jobs like extending a gangway, tunneling to another vein, or opening a new slope.

So the work and earnings of miners varied considerably from job to job, from mine to mine, and even from place to place in a mine. To add to the mine worker's worries, the consistency of his employment was dictated by the always unpredictable market for coal, with

***Mine Workers.*** *Miners blasted the coal face to extract large pieces, which laborers loaded on to cars.* ANTHRACITE HERITAGE MUSEUM

demand tending to peak in the late sum-mer and early fall as consumers prepared for winter, only to slacken thereafter. Many of the so-called company men who worked as bosses or as engine or pump operators or craftsmen could rely on rela-tively steady employment, since they per-formed basic maintenance and supervisory tasks needed even when demand declined. But miners and their laborers tended to face long days of labor followed within a few months by just a few partial days of work per week.

Just about any job in or around a mine was arduous, and those under-ground were especially dangerous. In addition to roof falls, underground work-ers had to worry about accumulations of bad air and natural gas, which could cause either suffocation or explosion. They also had to deal with the ever-present darkness, dissipated only by small oil lamps clipped onto the soft caps commonly worn in the early decades of mining. Workers aboveground did not face the same perils, but they had to deal with common industrial hazards, such as unguarded machinery that moved with a speed that could maim or kill, and boilers that could explode.

## EARLY LABOR STRUGGLES

Richard Sharpe assumed the primary burden of managing the Council Ridge mine for the twenty years of its first lease from the Coxes, especially so after the departure of John Leisenring in 1859 made the firm Sharpe, Weiss, and Company. Initially he faced two basic problems: supplying his customers and retaining his workers. The production of coal could not simply be turned on and off immediately at the customer's whim, and some workers were quick to depart if work seemed steadier at other mines. Still, the Council Ridge colliery and the Lehigh region coal trade in general experienced steady growth until the Civil War. Though that conflict depressed economic activity at first, it soon created a labor shortage. Asa Foster's son became a captain in Pennsylvania's 81st Regiment after the start of the war in 1861, and a good number of Eckley men went to war with him. The need for soldiers in the North only grew as the war heated up in 1862, and in late summer, the federal government required the states to draft men as the number of volunteers lagged.

To add to the tumult, opposition to the war was especially strong in the anthracite region. Irish-Americans generally favored the Democratic Party and offered relatively little support for the war led by Abraham Lincoln's Republicans. A number of protests occurred when military officials came to northeastern Pennsylvania to enroll men for the initial draft in the fall of 1862.

Throughout the anthracite region, operators, bosses, and public officials who showed enthusiasm for the draft or took strong measures against strikes received anonymous warnings of dire consequences if they did not mend their ways. One appeared in Eckley in October 1862, threatening the workers if they did not join in a protest against the draft. Similar threats throughout the anthracite fields were attributed to a mysterious group known as the Molly Maguires.

Initially labor relations in Eckley seemed less prone to conflict than elsewhere in the anthracite region, but no locality could escape the complex swirl of labor shortages, antiwar protest, work-related discontent, and budding efforts at labor organization. A comprehensive study of labor relations during the early years at Council Ridge reveals that the first substantial work stoppage at Eckley occurred in December 1863, when workers throughout the area refused to accept the customary wage reduction that operators imposed as demand declined once orders for winter had been filled. The operators relented soon after the first of the year, but the workers' success led the bosses to work together more closely. When employees demanded that the superintendent at Council Ridge fire an employee who had refused to join the recently formed union, an enraged Sharpe resisted the demand, and the workers went on strike. Local operators assisted Sharpe and his partners by complying with their request not to employ strikers and by continuing to supply Council Ridge's customers. With this support, Sharpe forced his men back to work.

These early skirmishes established the battle lines for the labor conflict that dominated the next decade at Council Ridge and across the anthracite region. Many workers tried to become better organized and get higher wages, while all sought sufficiently steady work to feed their families. Employers often joined together to weaken labor and keep wages down, while never ceasing to compete for business. At the root of the almost constant conflict was a problem that has plagued the coal industry, anthracite and bituminous, throughout its history: overproduction. To make maximum profit, mines expanded to supply the peak demand in summer and fall. But once that demand had been met, a mine couldn't simply close down to wait out the slow season that followed. Mines required extensive maintenance to stay open, but those costs were far less than the prohibitive ones involved in closing down a mine and trying to reopen it later. So once mines met peak demand, they generally kept producing at a somewhat lower level through the winter. Even if they produced coal for only five or six hours a day, two or three days a week, as was frequently done during the slack season, they remained ready to accelerate production whenever possible. The lengthy strikes that took place right after the Civil War, despite the rancor they generated, served to alleviate overproduction. Miners and operators noticed the rebound in coal prices after regional strikes of a month or two. A mine like Council Ridge, or even a company that owned many mines, would only cut its throat by limiting production on its own and thus surrendering its profit-making potential to competitors. But if production could be limited across the entire industry, prices could remain strong. To workers and their fledgling union, this meant that operators would not face the relentless pressure to save what money they could by cutting wages.

This was the great crusade of the first union to organize throughout the anthracite region, the Workingmen's Benevolent Association (WBA). In 1868 and 1869, it briefly exercised economic power on a scale never before seen in American labor, but in doing so, it caused mine operators to rise to defend what they saw as the most basic element of capitalism—their right to control their own businesses. The WBA began in Schuylkill County, and the impetus for its growth across the anthracite region was the passage of a state law that called for, but did not mandate, an eight-hour day for the state's workers starting on July 1, 1868. The union began a wave of strikes that day, demanding that operators not only accept the eight-hour day, but do so with no reduction in pay. Eckley workers did not join the strike until a committee came to town on July 10 to urge them to do so. At least some of the Eckley men were ready to return on July 23 but held back when a local man was murdered. While the motive for the crime was unclear, fear that it might have been some sort of reprisal kept Council Ridge idle until the beginning of August. Although this walkout did not accomplish its ambitious goals, it held out the prospect of unified action by workers across the entire industry, beyond the regional boundaries of the Schuylkill, Lehigh, and Wyoming fields.

Sharpe thought the WBA had little strength among his workers, but in May 1869 they formed a local and joined a strike rather than stay at work with the 10 percent advance offered by Sharpe. The purpose of this strike was to win a "basis" schedule of wages tied to coal prices, with a floor below which wages could not fall no matter how far prices might drop. By the end of the year, workers won the basis, but only after this strike and another one that began only weeks after the first ended. Altogether, labor conflict idled Council Ridge for more than one-third of 1869.

# WHO WERE THE MOLLY MAGUIRES?

No group in the history of the anthracite coal industry has attracted more attention than the Molly Maguires, from numerous books to a full-length feature film shot on the grounds of Eckley Miners' Village. But their goals and accomplishments are as shadowy as their identity. The substance of their legend reaches across the Atlantic to Ireland through centuries of British conquest and occupation. Irishmen who thought they had been wronged by the authorities stood little chance of success through open resistance. Many resorted to threats and attacks in secret against landlords, officials, and those they thought guilty of collaborating with British rule. Often they appeared disguised, even as women, leaving notices that warned foes to beware the wrath of the mythical "Molly Maguire" and her sons.

From 1846 to 1850, the potato famine in Ireland caused the deaths of one million and the emigration of one and a half million, with more than a million of those coming to America. A sizable proportion of these immigrants came to northeastern Pennsylvania to find work in the rapidly growing anthracite coal industry, and many of these came from the west of Ireland, where the tradition of Molly Maguire–style vio-

lence was especially strong. Most were desperately poor, and having little experience in mining, they obtained the worst jobs in the industry, often bossed by Englishmen and Welshmen who had preceded them in the coalfields. All of this reminded Irishmen of the oppression they had crossed the Atlantic to escape, and some turned to the age-old tradition of organized revenge.

Between June 1877 and December 1878, twenty men were hanged for a variety of murders and other crimes committed since 1862 in Schuylkill and Carbon Counties. These are the acts that constitute the crimes of the Molly Maguires. Some of those murdered were mine bosses, and some of those murders included the robbery of payrolls. Two of the earliest crimes were against bosses who confronted Irishmen protesting the Civil War draft. Other victims included a policeman and a Welsh miner who had run-ins with Irish miners. Some still dispute the guilt of a number of the defendants, especially those who were accused of conspiring in the crimes rather than actually carrying them out. Undercover operatives for the Pinkerton Detective Agency hired by the Philadelphia and Reading Railroad, in particular one James McParlan, infiltrated the Mollies through the Irish

With the mines closed for so much time, coal prices increased. Still, the specter of overproduction returned within a few months, and few coal operators could accept efforts by the WBA to limit production. The year 1870 was a good one at Council Ridge, but largely because a four-month strike in the Schuylkill region kept demand strong. Operators there achieved a reduction in the floor to which wages could fall with prices, and a strike against a wage reduction in the Wyoming region led the WBA to order a walkout for the entire industry in January 1871. This strike marked the beginning of the union's decline. It continued into May in the Wyoming and Schuylkill regions, with the northern men accepting severe

reductions and the southern men limiting them in a face-saving arbitration. Mine workers at Council Ridge and across the Lehigh region stayed out well into June before returning to work at a reduction of about 10 percent.

The WBA's short-lived success spurred the coal operators to organize, not only to resist the union, but also to try to control the price of coal. By 1873, the major coal companies were beginning the first in a long series of efforts to apportion the coal market and regulate production to keep prices high, none of which succeeded for long. In all of this, a firm like Sharpe, Weiss, and Company found itself in a difficult position. Independent of any transportation interests, the Council

*The Execution of Thomas Fisher, one of the Molly Maguires accused of murder. In addition to two vantage points of Fisher's hanging, this illustration shows portraits of (1) Morgan Powell, the man murdered, and (2) the accused Fisher.* ANTHRACITE HERITAGE MUSEUM

ethnic society, the Ancient Order of Hibernians, to which many of them belonged. The evidence McParlan supplied was essential for the convictions, but it has always been disputed by defenders of the Mollies.

The impact of the Mollies goes well beyond those specific crimes. Practically any act of violence in the anthracite region in the 1860s and 1870s directed against bosses or coal property was laid at their doorstep. This presents the most important issue for their legacy: Were the Mollies motivated by visions of social justice? In those years, the Workingmen's Benevolent Association was trying to build a strong union movement, and corporate officials linked the violence attributed to the Mollies to the union's growth. That strategy undoubtedly weakened the union, but in retrospect historians have found no clear links. Often the crimes for which the Mollies were convicted seem as much matters of personal revenge as any kind of organized labor radicalism.

Ridge operators had to make money on the coal they sold. Sharpe often criticized his more powerful business neighbors, such as Ario Pardee, the LCNC, and the Lehigh Valley Railroad, which controlled local and regional transportation links and sometimes limited the number of railroad cars they allotted to Eckley. On top of these problems, in 1873 the feverish prosperity of the post–Civil War era came crashing down in a financial panic, followed by the nation's first severe industrial depression.

While the WBA played no role in negotiations in the Wyoming region after 1871, in Lehigh and Schuylkill it managed to maintain wages with only small adjustments until 1875. But in the "long strike" of that year, which lasted from January into June, the operators handed the union its final defeat. The struggle was a bitter one, with violence near Eckley causing the state to send in militia troops in April. Gradually workers returned on their employers' terms, accepting sizable reductions in pay along with the removal of the floor for miners' wages, which could now fall fully in unison with coal prices. But one Eckley veteran, Richard Sharpe, missed the final act in the WBA struggle. Perhaps worn out by the many battles of the past twenty years, Sharpe left for Wilkes-Barre in November 1874, transferring his firm's lease to his former partner, John Leisenring.

## GROWING PRODUCTION, GROWING DANGER

The anthracite industry faced hard times for the rest of the 1870s. Although anthracite production rose overall, most mine workers experienced massive amounts of slack time, with the industry averaging fewer than 170 full days of work per year from 1876 through 1880. The 1880s were a steadier decade, and Council Ridge picked up the pace along with numerous other mines. John Leisenring had taken over the Council Ridge mines, but spent little time there, as he invested in bituminous mining properties in Pennsylvania and Virginia. Leisenring's son-in-law, Dr. John S. Wentz, served as superintendent. Under Wentz, the mines steadily produced more coal, exceeding 200,000 tons for the first time in 1881, surpassing 300,000 tons the following year, and reaching a peak of 409,000 tons in 1885. But with that level of production came a price: five fatal accidents at the Council Ridge mine that year. Previously, more than one or two a year had been unusual.

*Disaster in the Mines. As production rose at Council Ridge so too did mining accidents. In 1885 alone, five fatal accidents occurred at the colliery.* ANTHRACITE HERITAGE MUSEUM (HORGAN 15259)

Examining these fatalities provides a glimpse at the risks workers faced in this most dangerous of occupations. In 1870, the state of Pennsylvania took action to lessen those risks by initiating a program of inspection in the anthracite mines. State-appointed mine inspectors had the task of enforcing a long list of regulations against violations by operators and by workers, as well as reporting serious accidents that occurred. The state took action in the wake of a growing toll of accidents, most notably the Avondale disaster of 1869 south of Wilkes-Barre, in which 110 mine workers died in an explosion. Still, the intervention of the state could only limit the risk that mine workers faced.

Two of the victims at Eckley in 1885 died in collisions with coal cars. The youngest fatality was the fourteen-year-old mule driver's helper Peter McCue, who was crushed by a runaway coal car when a rope broke. Twenty-three-year-old laborer Michael Kochman was killed when he tried to ride on a moving coal car but slipped between cars and was crushed. August Whitbread, a thirty-four-year-old miner, died five days after he was hit by a fall of coal, the most common kind of mining accident. When miner Michael Lludner was setting his powder cartridge deep into the coal before blasting, the cartridge became stuck, and instead of drilling it out and starting all over again as state mining regulations dictated, he rammed the cartridge, causing it to explode. Thomas Denneny, a thirty-eight-year-old miner, died from burns caused by a gas explosion. His place in the mines had not been inspected for gas, as state law required.

Before 1915, Pennsylvania had no workers compensation law to pay benefits to injured workers or to the families of those killed on the job. Few mine workers could obtain or afford private insurance, and few companies paid any substantial benefits. So the families of workers killed in the mines had two choices: sue the company for negligence or rely on charities, if available. Workers' families had difficulty winning suits against employers. Even those with good cases often settled for sums ranging from several hundred dollars for a young worker to about a thousand for a husband or father. The families of workers whose negligence contributed to the accident generally had no case. They were lucky to receive a period of free rental for their company house, a break in their company store bill, burial expenses, or free coal for the winter. In an isolated place like Eckley, widows could not get jobs. Instead they resorted to taking in boarders, selling alcohol illegally, or begging to support their families. If they had boys, they sent them to the mines to work, relying on lax enforcement of Pennsylvania's child labor statute, which by 1885 prohibited boys under twelve from working on the surface and those under fourteen from working underground.

## ECKLEY B. COXE

At the end of 1885, the mines at Eckley for the first time came under the management of the family that had owned the land for about a century, the Coxes. The land purchased in the 1780s by the economic theorist and government official, Tench Coxe, had been held by his son, Philadelphia attorney and judge Charles S. Coxe, whose growing family spent summers on their land in southern Luzerne County. The partners who operated the Council Ridge mine rented the land, first known informally as Shingletown, from the Coxes and paid them royalties for the coal removed. But the partners' decision in 1857 to name their mining town Eckley, after the original choice of Fillmore had been turned down by the post office, hinted at the vital role to be played by Eckley Brinton Coxe.

Born on June 4, 1839, in Philadelphia, Eckley Coxe was the second son and middle child of seven. Like many other sons of the well-to-do in this era, he began his college education earlier than is the custom today, entering the University of Pennsylvania at fifteen in 1854 and graduating four years later. By the time the village of Eckley was named after him, he had begun to show an interest in the coal industry, accompanying his father on visits to the family's coal properties. In 1860, his pursuit of a career in mining took him to Europe to study in leading technical schools and visit mines there.

Few Americans could rival young Eckley Coxe's intensive study of mining by the time he returned home and founded Coxe Brothers and Company in January 1865. Soon thereafter, the firm opened its first mine at Drifton, about five miles from Eckley, and proceeded to open a number of other mines and gradually take control of the family's leased properties. Coxe Brothers took over the mine at Council Ridge and the village of Eckley at the end of 1885, as the lease of Leisenring and Company expired. By that point, Coxe Brothers had become the largest independent producer in the anthracite industry—one not controlled by a railroad—at more than one million tons of coal a year.

Eckley Brinton Coxe is one of those few individuals whose breadth of interests made them deserving of the title of Renaissance man. He knew French, Latin, and German, and could use the last well enough to translate an important engineering text for publication. His appreciation for learning is reflected in his service as a founding trustee of Lehigh University and his establishment of the Mining and Mechanical Institute. Originally a night school for mine workers founded in 1879 in Drifton, today it

*Eckley B. Coxe, cofounder of Coxe Brothers and Company, state senator, technical innovator, and philanthropist.* ECKLEY MINERS' VILLAGE

prepares young people for higher education in the nearby town of Freeland. His technological imagination can be seen in the numerous patents he received, many of which came from his most impressive technical achievement, building the first coal breaker made of iron and steel rather than wood. The high quality of work at the company's shops in Drifton lured the inventor Thomas Edison to visit in 1891. In 1880, Coxe helped establish the American Society of Mechanical Engineers, still an important professional organization, and he became its president in 1893.

Coxe's talent could not long avoid the political spotlight, and he won election to the state senate in 1880. However, displaying uncommon moral rectitude, he refused to take the oath of office because it required him to swear that all contributions to his campaign had been given as "expressly authorized by law." While he informed his constituents he knew of nothing inappropriate in his fund raising, he would not take office since he could not verify the legality of every contribution. He made sure that he could do so in his next campaign and won by a far larger majority. Although he was mentioned as a possible candidate for governor and led the state's delegation to the Democratic National Convention in 1884, he displayed little political ambition, leaving the state senate after his second term.

Although Coxe may well have set a higher standard for integrity than many of the business leaders of the late nineteenth century, when the United States took over world economic leadership from the nations of Europe, he shared a fundamental belief with most of his fellow businessmen—opposition to trade unions. Coxe prided himself on resolving disputes with his workers, but for him that stopped short of negotiating with regional and national unions and their officials. He maintained a united front with other Lehigh field operators like John Markle and Ario Pardee, defeating two allied unions in one of the longest strikes in the history of the industry, from September 1887 to March 1888. Congress held hearings to investigate, and Coxe showed no regrets about the strike, stating, "As I have said over and over again it does not worry me. When I had the first strike it almost made me sick. It is like a man when his first child has a tooth, he thinks it is dreadful, but when his third child has the fifteenth tooth he does not think so much of it." He told the committee that he disliked the traditional company town practice of the company deducting from the workers' pay not only for their store bill, but also for services from a doctor, a priest, or a butcher. His company had discontinued all such collections, paying its men in cash once rent was deducted. If a worker failed to pay his store bill, the company would not let him accumulate debt, though it would allow him to continue to buy in case of illness.

Coxe did not hesitate to discuss economic conditions in the industry. Success required careful attention to detail and vigorous competition with the large railroad companies, who could turn a profit on their charges for transporting coal to market. Although Coxe might have exaggerated when he maintained that "out of every hundred operators that have gone into the business I do not suppose there is 10 percent of them who have made anything," his comments hint at the stresses that by the 1920s would initiate the industry's long, slow decline.

Eckley B. Coxe died on May 13, 1895, a few weeks before his fifty-fifth birthday. His mines closed for several days in tribute, and all of the area's mines ceased operating on the day of his funeral. His direct influence over Eckley's workers lasted for less than ten years. Still, he established an influential legacy, not only through his many technical innovations, but also by his philanthropic efforts and those of his wife, Sophia Georgianna Coxe. His company was one of the few that provided a benefit plan for workers injured or killed in accidents. Perhaps because she had no children of her own, Mrs. Coxe focused on improving the lives of the children of mine workers. While overseas with her husband in 1889, she learned of a treatment for diphtheria, which took the lives of so many infants in this era, and brought it back to help local families. She frequently traveled through the mining villages, checking on the injured and sick and providing them nursing care and medical supplies. She made sure that families with young children received deliveries of milk. She funded expansion of Hazleton State Hospital, White Haven Sanitarium, and the Mining and Mechanical Institute. As many children of mine workers have recalled, she gave Christmas gifts to children of employees and hosted an annual Christmas party. One worker reflected in an oral history interview that the anthracite region would have been a far better place "if every one of these coal operators would do just one part of what the Coxes did."

## THE STRUGGLE FOR THE UNION

Whether or not an employer showed philanthropic kindness, workers quickly realized that their employer's first concern was his own business. Anthracite mine workers knew that they had little bargaining power in individual negotiations with their employer and came to realize that joined together they might win a better deal. Thus mine workers, especially immigrants with different languages and cultures, listened carefully when organizers for the nation's leading miners' union, the United Mine Workers of America (UMWA), came to the anthracite fields in the 1890s.

Eckley's men joined in the strike that swept the Lehigh coalfield after one of the most horrifying episodes in American labor history, the Lattimer Massacre of September 10, 1897. On that day, sheriff's deputies fired indiscriminately into a crowd of unarmed miners, who were already on strike, to stop them from marching into the company town of Lattimer Mines, owned by local operator Calvin Pardee, to persuade those workers to walk out too. Outrage over the death of some nineteen workers and the wounding of thirty-six in the incident, almost all of whom were Slovakian and Polish immigrants, led to the organization of UMWA District Seven for the Lehigh region.

*Lattimer, 1897. Strikers march toward Lattimer to close the mines. Shortly beyond this point, they will confront a posse that will open fire and kill nineteen of their members.*

The union made only limited progress until 1900, when its national headquarters sent a cadre of organizers through the anthracite fields. Their efforts gave the union enough confidence to call a strike in September that lasted six weeks. That walkout involved all of the anthracite fields for the first time since 1871. The men returned with a wage increase of 10 percent, but the coal operators refused to recognize the union, setting the stage for one of the most important battles between labor and capital in American history, the anthracite coal strike of 1902.

By 1902, the UMWA had enrolled about half of the 150,000 mine workers employed in the anthracite industry. With such a strong organization, the UMWA believed itself ready for a showdown with the anthracite operators, led by the presidents of several major eastern railroads that operated a sizable proportion of the industry's mines and provided transportation for most of the rest. Like Richard Sharpe and Eckley Coxe before them, those presidents wanted to get rid of the union. The UMWA demanded a wage increase of approximately 20 percent, along with a reduction in the work day from ten to eight hours, as well as recognition of the union. A few meetings took place between railroad presidents and union leaders, but they accomplished little. On May 12, practically all anthracite mine workers walked off their jobs, not to return for some five and a half months, on October 23. Despite massive fund-raising efforts by the union to help supply the strikers, workers and their families were clearly stretched to the limits of their endurance. They went back to work when President Theodore Roosevelt offered to establish a panel of experts, the Anthracite Coal Strike Commission, to investigate the industry and rule on the mine workers' demands. The president took this action, welcomed by the union but only grudgingly accepted by the railroad presidents, to allay growing fear over rising fuel prices as winter and the national congressional elections approached. Significantly, Roosevelt's summoning of the commission marked the first time the federal government intervened in a labor dispute in some way other than sending troops to break a strike, as the railroad presidents had urged him to do.

The commission met for more than three months of hearings, calling hundreds of witnesses, ranging from coal company officials to miners. One witness was an Eckley miner named Mike

Midlick. A strong union man, Midlick spent much of his time telling the commission of the day-to-day grievances he had as a miner for Coxe Brothers. After completing their deliberations, the commission handed down a compromise settlement that included a wage increase of about 10 percent and a reduction in hours of work from ten to nine. While the commission did not require the coal operators to recognize the UMWA, it did set up a Board of Conciliation where future disputes between workers and management could be settled by their representatives.

The Board of Conciliation had a great deal of work to do in the aftermath of the strike and settlement, and one of the companies that appeared most often before the board was Coxe Brothers and its longtime mining superintendent, Edgar Kudlich. Coxe Brothers and its men argued over such issues as the reinstatement of strikers, interpretation of the reduction of hours clause in the settlement, and such disputes as the firing of one worker who called another a "sonofabitch." Throughout the anthracite industry, recourse to the Board of Conciliation made strikes less likely and labor relations less hostile, if not exactly friendly. Management and union representatives met on a regular basis, and though big walkouts continued to occur, especially in the 1920s, the framework provided by the commission's settlement and the board's rulings kept lines of communication open. Just as important, the presence of the union, even in company towns like Eckley, gave workers a voice that could not be ignored.

## TWENTIETH-CENTURY LIFE
The struggle for unionization was just one more step toward the goal that had brought men across the Atlantic to Eckley since the 1850s—economic security for themselves and their families. By the early decades of the twentieth century, many of the families from England, Wales, and Ireland who had come to the town one or two generations previously had moved on, replaced by recent immigrants from Eastern Europe. Most of them came from agricultural villages in the foothills of the Tatra Mountains, in what today is northern Slovakia and southern Poland. Before World War I, both of those lands were part of the Austro-Hungarian Empire. The immigrants usually were not the poorest of the poor, but from families who owned small plots of land. In the last half of the nineteenth century, they increasingly struggled to hold enough land to maintain viable farms for their growing extended families. To buy more land, they needed cash, which they sought by sending family members, sons in particular, to find industrial work. Their search for jobs would take them across Europe and eventually to the rapidly industrializing United States.

Work in coal mines holds little appeal to most of us in the twenty-first century. But despite all of the danger and insecurity that surrounded it, such work gave immigrants a chance not only to earn enough money to survive in places like Eckley, but to save some to send home. To do so, workers kept their expenses at a minimum by living with relatives or acquaintances as boarders, paying small sums for food and lodging. Early in the twentieth century, a little less than 10 percent of Eckley's population were boarders, most of them in homes with other workers. While this may seem to be a large proportion compared with communities today, it was smaller than in many larger industrial towns with a greater variety of housing. To make economic progress, a boarder working in the anthracite coal mines first had to avoid unemployment and

*Main Street of Eckley, c. 1900.*
ECKLEY MINERS' VILLAGE

injury. An adult immigrant might begin as a laborer for a miner, loading coal for perhaps $1.50 per day. The crucial step toward a higher income was to obtain a more lucrative job as a miner. To do that, a miner's laborer needed his miner's certificate, required by the state beginning in 1889 to make the mines safer and to slow the progress of immigrants into miners' jobs. After two years of experience, a laborer could get his certificate by passing an oral examination of twelve questions in English given by a board of experienced miners, though some could obtain a certificate illegally. Although the most highly skilled miners could earn as much as $4 or $5 a day on a reasonably steady basis, the new immigrant miner was more likely to struggle for some time at $2 or $3 a day while facing as many as a hundred days of enforced idleness per year, due to the chronic underemployment that continued to plague the anthracite industry in the 1890s and early 1900s.

Eastern European immigrants commonly returned home several times, some for good, but more than half eventually put down roots in America. Eckley remained a community dominated by the foreign-born and their children well into the twentieth century. In 1900, only 10 percent of its residents were native-born children of native-born parents. The rest of the population were, in roughly equal proportions, foreign-born or the children of immigrants. By 1920, the percentage of native-born children of native-born parents had increased only slightly, while a bit under 30 percent of the population had been born overseas. By that year, more than half of Eckley's residents were the children of immigrants.

To obtain the margin needed for a relatively stable working-class life in America early in the twentieth century, a family had to find ways to add to the father's earnings. The income of one adult male breadwinner making $2 to $3 per day when steadily employed merely enabled a family to survive. In mining communities, boys might go to work in and around the mines as early as seven or eight, though by 1900 the increased availability of schooling and efforts to enforce child labor laws were beginning to increase that age. Boarders provided vital income for the families who cared for them in their homes. Some families might have as many as six to eight boarders, though it was more common to have two to three. Wives and daughters helped earn that income by cooking meals, washing clothes, and tending to gardens and barnyard animals in the spacious backyards. Children helped by picking pieces of coal for household use from the growing waste banks that dotted the countryside. Women were prohibited by both state law and tradition from working in the mines, but they could walk several miles to take a trolley to nearby towns for jobs in garment and textile factories. With the daughters working either in or outside of the home and the sons at the mines, families could double what the father earned.

It is no easy task to visualize today how crowded a place Eckley was in the early 1900s. From the 1880s, it held nearly two hundred houses, expanding along Main Street and the parallel Back Street (also called South Street) away from the better homes in the western part of town. Since Eckley was never incorporated, its lack of legal boundaries makes various population figures tricky to interpret. According to one estimate, Eckley reached a population peak of approximately fifteen hundred in 1885, when the expansion of mining in the last years of the Leisenring lease brought more than seven hundred workers to its mine. Data from the 1880 census, however, gave a figure of just under eleven hundred, and calculations from the 1900 census yield a little over eleven hundred. The average household size in Eckley in the 1900 census was about six persons, with as many as twelve or more at some addresses that were one side of the double homes that predominated. So approximately twelve people commonly lived in those double homes, and twenty or more might reside in some of them. But compared with urban industrial areas like Pittsburgh or Philadelphia, there was plenty of room, especially to garden and keep some animals on the fifty-by-two-hundred-foot lots. In the summer, life would spill out of the house, with people staying outside for as much time as they could.

Life in Eckley combined hardships that are hard to imagine with a sense of community difficult to re-create today. Much of what generated that sense of community was the sharing of hardships, especially in a company town like Eckley, where life varied so little for so many of its residents. Most of the houses were the one-and-a-half-story double houses still seen along Main Street today, but some residents lived in even smaller dwellings along Back Street, which no longer

remain. Most houses in town got electrical service in the 1920s, but many lacked indoor toilets or hot water until years later. While the company store reflects the limited range of choices life in Eckley offered, former residents fondly recall the store, after the company no longer owned it, allowing workers to buy on credit, even during strikes. The town's isolation is reflected in that the Coxes closed down its only bar when they took over management of Eckley. Recreation was simple, but nonetheless memorable. Children had plenty of room to play in the woods beyond the town, and families often went on picnics and even picked berries in the surrounding woods. On nearby ballfields, teams from the various mining towns competed.

Eckley had only a limited number of community institutions and services. But that lack of variety brought people together, whether they liked it or not, making life in the company town an oddly egalitarian socializing experience for wave after wave of new arrivals, or "greenhorns." For most families in Eckley, there was one church, the Roman Catholic Church of the Immaculate Con-

***Children at Eckley***, *despite the hardships of mining life, were able to find time to play in the nearby woods.* ECKLEY MINERS' VILLAGE

ception, located on the east end of town, just beyond the town's least distinguished homes. The St. James Episcopal Church and the Presbyterian church were on the other side of town, serving very different and much smaller congregations. The children of Welsh and English Episcopalians and Presbyterians might attend the schools that met in each of those churches, but most of Eckley's young people attended the one-room school built soon after the town was settled. It was later upgraded to a four-room school, and in 1912, it was replaced by a more modern two-story, six-room structure that stood where the Visitor Center does today, closing in 1948.

Eckley's isolation gradually broke down during the twentieth century. Outside vendors increasingly came into town selling fresh meat, beer, and other products from their carts far into most evenings. Some workers walked several miles to work at nearby mines or to go to one of the few places in the area that was not a company town, Freeland, its name announcing its noncompany status. Many Eastern European immigrants walked to churches there to worship with others of their nationality. From Freeland, one could get on a trolley to have access to a much wider world. Rail service was not as cheap or as frequent, but it, too, provided a way out. By the 1920s, automobiles had become a bit more common around the town. Very few workers had one, but even a small number of cars increased mobility. Perhaps more important, the advent of radio opened a window on the world for workers and their families without necessitating long trips. With more and more Eckley residents born in the United States and educated here, even if for just a few years, their horizons greatly expanded beyond those of their immigrant parents. Like previous generations of immigrants' children, many soon moved on to places where they could at least have the hope of buying their own homes.

*The Church was an important symbol of ethnic identity for immigrant miners and their families. This Presbyterian church served the English and Welsh communities at Eckley.* ECKLEY MINERS' VILLAGE

## THE DECLINE OF ANTHRACITE

The lifting of Eckley's isolation coincided with decreasing economic opportunity in Eckley and throughout the anthracite coal industry. Already by 1900, production at Eckley included substantial strip mining—using steam shovels to tear hundreds of feet of earth off coal seams so they could be mined from above. Much of the strip mining occurred to the southeast of Eckley on the property of the Buck Mountain colliery, purchased by Eckley B. Coxe at the same time he took over management of the Council Ridge colliery. With the expansion of operations around Buck Mountain, production continued at about two hundred thousand tons per year. With the strong demand for anthracite in the 1910s, production at Eckley reached and exceeded three hundred thousand tons per year a number of

*Eckley Miners, c. 1940.* ECKLEY MINERS' VILLAGE

times. Personal control of the property by the Coxe family had ended in 1905, when several of Eckley's brothers sold out to the Lehigh Valley Railroad. Population remained relatively stable in the town during these years, at around a thousand.

For the anthracite industry overall, production hit its peak in 1917 at just under one hundred million tons. But no one could realize that the 1920s would be the beginning of the end, as anthracite mining embarked on a long decline from which it has never recovered. Strip mining increasingly dominated the industry, just as it had at Eckley. It saved money for coal operators, but at the price of providing fewer jobs for workers and damaging the environment so extensively that Pennsylvanians today are still dealing with that damage, visible and invisible. The expansion of production for World War I went far beyond peacetime demand in the twenties at the same time that anthracite experienced growing competition from oil and gas heat. Strikes just as long as the 1902 walkout hit the industry in 1922 and 1925, having a serious impact on both workers and consumers. By the 1930s, anthracite production had plummeted below sixty million tons a year, and in those Depression years, mine workers lucky enough to have jobs worked only about half of the year. World War II sparked several years of increased production, but the industry's collapse proceeded rapidly after war's end. By 1960, production had fallen below twenty million tons mined by fewer than thirty thousand workers. In just a little over forty years, the anthracite industry had declined 80 percent in both production and employment.

The ongoing expansion of strip mining enabled production at Eckley to remain steadier than for the industry as a whole. Annual production exceeded three hundred thousand tons into the 1940s and two hundred thousand tons for several years in the 1950s. But all of this production did not mean growth or even stability for the town. More and more of the land in and around Eckley was stripped away, destroying a number of the houses on the property. Population figures become even more sketchy after 1920, but by the 1960s, the town had surely fallen below five hundred. Symbolic of Eckley's decline is the decision by the post office in 1957 to close down its office in Eckley, one hundred years after establishing the town's first post office had required changing its name from Fillmore to Eckley.

By the 1960s, the anthracite coal region had become one of the most depressed areas of the United States. While the term had not yet been invented, the counties of northeastern and east-central Pennsylvania where miners and entrepreneurs had once clamored for coal's riches now suffered from a relentless process of "deindustrialization." By the 1960s, Eckley seemed condemned to one of two fates: destruction of the town to strip-mine what coal remained under it or, if no market remained for such coal, slow, gradual abandonment as this company town lost its reason for existence.

## THE CREATION OF
## ECKLEY MINERS' VILLAGE

That a Hollywood film could save a coal company town serves as a kind of metaphor for America's changing economy, from providing daily necessities for people to creating a multitude of more visible but less essential services that our ancestors only dreamed of a hundred years ago. No product was more fundamental to the rise of American industry than anthracite coal, while movies are at the heart of an industry—the entertainment industry—whose influence today would surely amaze those practical-minded ancestors. It was the decision of Paramount Pictures in the late 1960s to make a movie about the most notorious episode in the history of the anthracite coal industry, The Molly Maguires, that saved Eckley from destruction and resulted in the Pennsylvania Historical and Museum Commission's decision to preserve and operate it as Eckley Miners' Village. Paramount chose Eckley as its primary location for filming for two reasons. First, Eckley still looked much like an anthracite coal town from about the 1870s. Second, Eckley was still owned and operated as a company town and had never been, like so many others, sold off bit by bit to its residents. Consequently, Paramount only had to get permission to film from the owner, George Huss. It cost $8 million to make The Molly Maguires, rather a big-budget effort for that day. About 40 percent of that sum was spent in and around Hazleton, with a great deal spent in Eckley during filming there in 1968. Paramount had a replica of the outer shell of a wooden coal breaker built for $200,000 and paid more than $100,000 to put telephone lines underground. Other ways in which the town was restored to more of a nineteenth-century look included removing shrubs and trees, covering electric meters, and putting wooden siding over houses that had been covered with modern materials. For the inconvenience they had to deal with, the community's eighty-six residents received six months of free rent.

On January 27, 1970, The Molly Maguires, starring Richard Harris, King Arthur in Camelot, and Sean Connery, well known for his role as secret agent James Bond, premiered at the Feeley Theater in Hazleton. The film received critical acclaim but lost money at the box office. Because of the attention the film focused on it, however, Eckley would be preserved in a far more effective way than on celluloid alone. While the movie was being completed, a group affiliated with the Hazleton Chamber of Commerce raised $100,000 to purchase the town. On the day of the premiere, that group, the Anthracite Historic Site and Museum Corporation, presented Eckley to the state of Pennsylvania with

# PATCH TOWN DAYS

Patch Town Days is one of the annual events at Eckley. Participants dress in coal mining attire and demonstrate the work practices and day-to-day routines of the Eckley community. Contact the site for more information on the event and on other programs held throughout the year (see page 47).

the hope, realized in 1975, that it would become one of several museum sites commemorating and interpreting the history of the anthracite coal industry.

As much as Eckley seems to be a piece of another time, the historic site that is Eckley Miners' Village is a dynamic effort to preserve its history through ongoing restoration, interpretation, and public educational programs. Like the thousands of workers who made a living in Eckley over the years only to move on, impelled by the forces of economic change, historic sites cannot stand still and must constantly look for new ways to tell an old story. But all of those new ways must begin with the unique resource preserved here. The buildings of Eckley Miners' Village surround visitors with what no virtual imagery can duplicate—the living artifact of a real town. With that reality all around them, visitors can begin to imagine and understand what life was like here.

# SITE LEGEND

1 Visitor Center

2 Picnic Area

3 Immaculate Conception Church Rectory and Museum Store+

4 The Church of the Immaculate Conception*

5 Laborers' Double Dwelling

6 Foundations of Double Dwellings

7 Back (or South) Street Cottage*

8 Laborers' Double Dwelling

9 Eckley Sports and Social Club

10 Miners' Double Dwelling*

11 Double Family Dwelling*

12 Mule Barn Movie Prop

13 Company Store Movie Prop*

14 Breaker Movie Prop

15 Single Family Dwelling

16 Presbyterian Church Site

17 St. James Episcopal Church*

18 Foundation of Eckley Hotel

19 Doctor's Office*

20 Site of Company Store

21 Mine Owner's House

22 Mule Barn

23 Feed Barn

[restrooms symbol] Restrooms

*Guided tours only

+Open Memorial Day to October 31

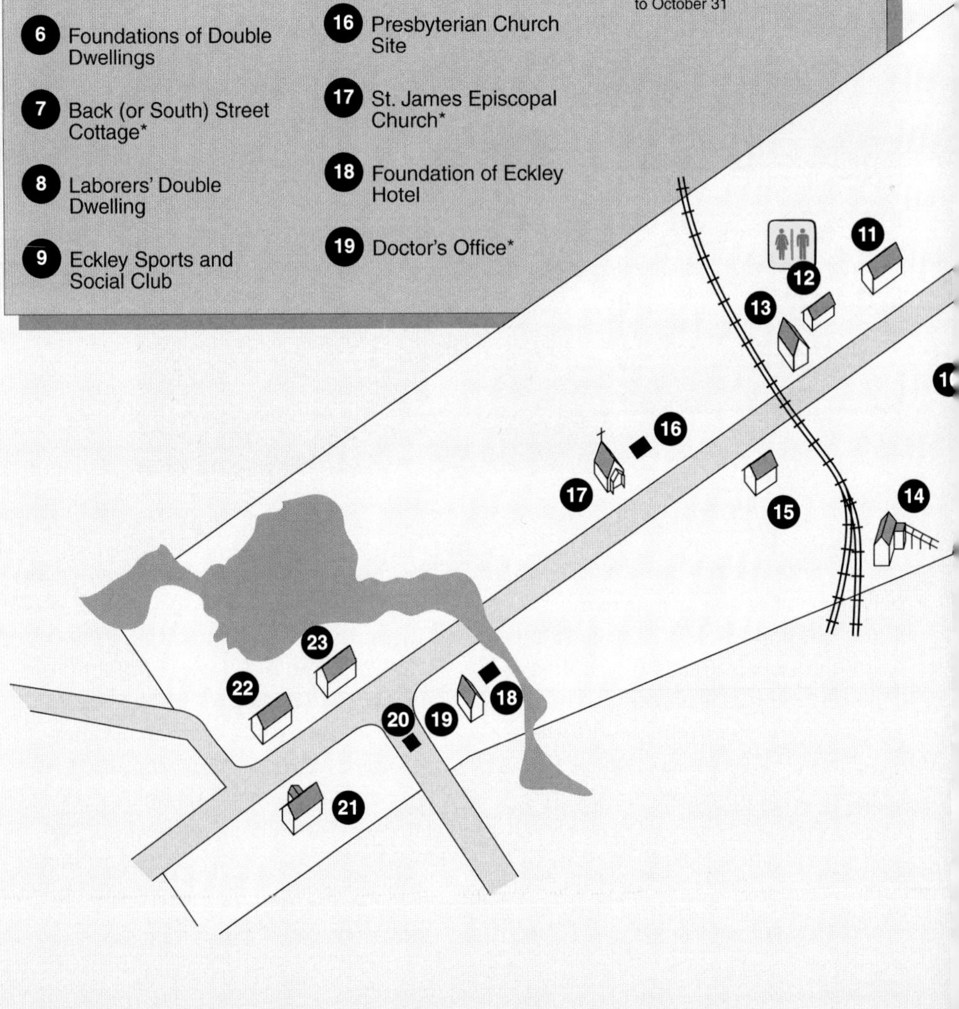

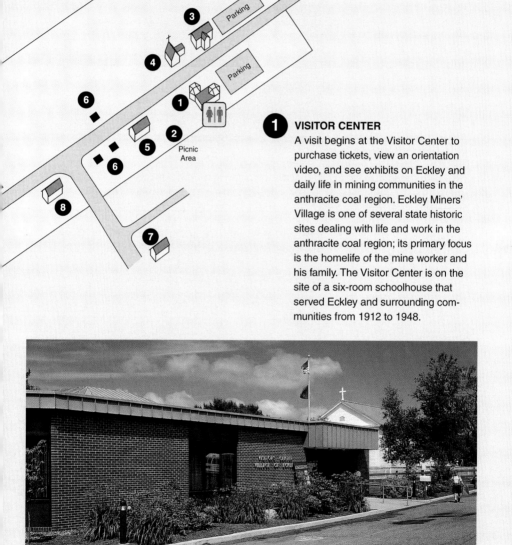

Parking

Parking

Picnic Area

### VISITOR CENTER

A visit begins at the Visitor Center to purchase tickets, view an orientation video, and see exhibits on Eckley and daily life in mining communities in the anthracite coal region. Eckley Miners' Village is one of several state historic sites dealing with life and work in the anthracite coal region; its primary focus is the homelife of the mine worker and his family. The Visitor Center is on the site of a six-room schoolhouse that served Eckley and surrounding communities from 1912 to 1948.

### 3 IMMACULATE CONCEPTION CHURCH RECTORY, 1861

The Catholic church and its rectory, or priest's residence, was placed at the eastern end of town, as far as possible from the residences of the mine operators and the Protestant churches they attended. Catholics dominated the lower ranks of Eckley's workforce, and housing for those workers was placed at the east side of town near the rectory and church. The rectory, built in the Gothic Revival style, served as the residence of parish priests Father Patrick J. Noonan (1862–68), Father John Mullen (1868–69), and Father Michael Fallihee (1870–1902). In 1902, when the Church of the Immaculate

Conception was downgraded to mission status, losing its resident priest, the rectory became a private home. This building now houses the Museum Store.

### 4 THE CHURCH OF THE IMMACULATE CONCEPTION, 1861

When mining began at Eckley, a majority of its workers were Irish and Catholic. The Coxes deeded land for the church to the Catholic Diocese of Philadelphia. The altar was consecrated by the diocese's archbishop, James Frederic Wood, on October 25, 1861. The church began as a mission church but soon became a parish church with the appointment of Father Noonan as Eckley's first pastor in 1862. In 1868, the parish became part of the newly organized Diocese of Scranton. In the village's early decades, the mine operators deducted 50 cents from the

pay of each mine worker for the support of the priest.

As more and more Eastern European Catholics immigrated to Eckley in the 1880s and 1890s, many of them preferred to worship at churches with others of their own nationality. Once several such churches were organized in the nearby noncompany town of Freeland, attendance at Immaculate Conception declined. In 1902, St. Ann's Church in Freeland received parish status, and Immaculate Conception moved to mission status. Mass continued to be celebrated at Immaculate Conception into the early 1960s, but with Eckley's population declining rapidly, the church was deconsecrated.

The church has its original altar and has been restored to its appearance as of the 1920s. Church furnishings other than the altar are from other Catholic churches in the area, in particular the Church of the Immaculate Conception in Berwick, Columbia County.

### 5 LABORERS' DOUBLE DWELLING, c. 1854

Houses like this one at the eastern end of the village were generally occupied by unskilled laborers. Each family in the double house had two rooms upstairs and two downstairs, with a shallow stone cellar in which food from the garden could be preserved and stored. Like all of Eckley's company houses, these are plank frame houses, with walls made of a series of long wooden planks covered on the outside by clapboards and on the interior with plaster.

### 6 FOUNDATIONS OF DOUBLE DWELLINGS

These show the stone foundations that even the smallest Eckley houses had, as well as the amount of room between them. Many of the company houses of all the varied types have been destroyed over the years. At Eckley's peak of population in the 1880s, there were nearly two hundred houses in the village.

### 7 BACK (OR SOUTH) STREET COTTAGE, c. 1854

Double houses like this one were the smallest in Eckley, with only three rooms for each family. This street once had thirty-two of these houses. Like the houses nearby on Main Street, these were generally occupied by unskilled laborers. The houses were made the cheapest way possible, of board-and-batten construction in which the exterior was only one layer of board thick rather than two.

## 8 LABORERS' DOUBLE DWELLING, c. 1854

With the exterior removed, you can view the plank frame building technique used in Eckley company houses. Despite its many limitations from our current-day perspective, it at least had a double thickness of boards, making these houses more weathertight than the board-and-batten cottages around the corner on Back (or South) Street. Plank framing was the common method of construction for houses before balloon framing, which was just coming into use when Eckley was built and resembles much of today's home construction. In balloon framing, vertical pieces of timber, one-and-a-half to two feet apart, are nailed to horizontal pieces at both the floor and roof lines, as opposed to the solid, if thin, wood walls in these plank-framed houses. The small rectangular opening in the house's foundation is a chute leading to a coal bin in the cellar.

## 9 ECKLEY SPORTS AND SOCIAL CLUB, 1946

This clubhouse was built by men from Eckley in 1946 with permission of the Coxe estate, which retained control of the property, and the Eckley Sports and Social Club was chartered in 1947. The Coxe family had long forbidden the sale of "spirituous or vinous intoxicating liquor," so no alcohol could be served at the club. Although the building was a mid-twentieth-century addition to the village, Paramount Pictures filmed the exterior as the Emerald House, the pub in which members of the Molly Maguires gathered.

### 10 MINERS' DOUBLE DWELLING, c. 1854

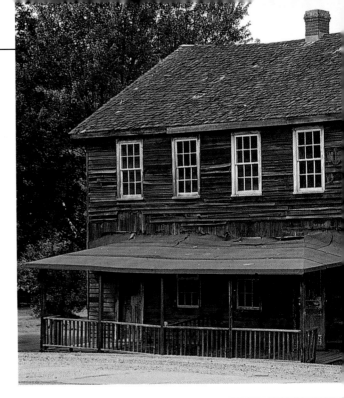

In Eckley, houses generally became bigger the farther one moved toward the western end of town, where the mine operators lived during the early years of the village. This house is typical of those that miners and their families occupied. Like some of the laborers' houses, this double house has two rooms upstairs and two rooms downstairs for each family, but it also has some attic space. In the 1850s, homes like these rented for $2.66 per month. Red and black were typically used as exterior colors in this era, with red being the cheapest pigment available.

Exhibits on the first floor of each side of the house show the typical furnishings of mine workers at two common stages of their working lives: as recent immigrants in the 1880s and as established miners after ten years or so of residence. Recent immigrants tended to experience the most crowded conditions, with large families and often a few boarders. The priorities were survival and then savings, perhaps for family members who remained in the old country, at a time when their income from mining tended to be lowest. Thus they struggled to get by with the most limited and basic implements. Prominent here is a cast-iron stove from the 1840s, typical in that recent immigrants would have had to make do with an old appliance they could obtain cheaply. The stove not only was used to

cook the family's food, but also was the only source of heat for the entire house.

Not on display, but of critical importance to mine workers' lives, was a metal washtub in which the men bathed in the kitchen with water brought into the house and heated in kettles. This is one of the many tasks that occurred outside in the summer shanty that can be seen behind the house next door, which also served as an addition to the kitchen. Imagine the hubbub of a husband and several sons in succession having their baths after a dirty day in the mines, with a wife and daughters

attending them while trying to begin preparing dinner too. The one decoration on display, showing the personal role of religion in immigrants' lives, is a print of St. Nicholas.

The miner and his wife generally slept in a downstairs bedroom like this one representing the lives of recent immigrants, which again illustrates just how basic their furnishings were. Other than a bed with its mattress supported by ropes, often an immigrant couple's proudest possession, there is only a barrel and a wooden box that once held dynamite used as a nightstand. The only decoration is a religious print. It was uncommon for a family beginning life in America to have more than one bed, but crowded conditions forced them to use every bit of sleeping space, with children and boarders often sleeping on pallets covered by straw.

The ability of an immigrant family to acquire possessions after a decade or so of reasonably steady work can be seen in the rooms of the house next door. The kitchen has a newer, more efficient stove, along with an array of kitchen implements ranging from a coffee grinder and pots and pans to crockery and kettles. The miner's lunch pail is evidence of a family that no longer needs to improvise, and the copper washtub must have been both functional and durable. One can imagine the family's pride in its table and chairs, and the sense of accomplishment of the woman of the house when she acquired the sewing machine. One other bit of evidence of growing gentility is that the religious prints in the kitchen are framed. Similarly, the bedroom shows people striving for a few comforts. The three religious prints here are framed, each located over an important piece of furniture: the bed, a table, and a chest of drawers. Basic amenities like the rag rugs on

the floor, the two chairs, and the kerosene lamp show the struggle of the miner and his

family to bring the homey feel of the Victorian age into their remote coal company town.

**11** **DOUBLE FAMILY DWELLING, c. 1875**

Although most of the houses in Eckley were built in the village's first years, some, like this home, were built years later. Houses like this one were for miners or other skilled workers, as were those constructed earlier across the street.

**12** **MULE BARN MOVIE PROP**

This is one of several structures built in 1968 as props for the film *The Molly Maguires.* The original barn has been rebuilt at the western end of town.

### 13 COMPANY STORE MOVIE PROP

This structure was built in 1968 as a prop for *The Molly Maguires*. The original store site was located at the western end of town, near the better homes in which mine operators and bosses lived.

### 14 BREAKER MOVIE PROP

Constructed for the movie in 1968, this building's exterior resembles the wooden breakers that dominated the anthracite region in the middle decades of the 1800s. Coxe Brothers and Company, owners of Eckley, built the industry's first iron breaker in 1895. In the breaker, most of the colliery's aboveground workforce was involved in separating slate, rock, and dirt from the coal, while massive rollers broke big pieces of coal into smaller sizes more desired by the consumer. Most of the workers at the breaker were the slate pickers or breaker boys, who, as young as seven or eight years of age in the 1800s, sat astride coal chutes where anthracite rushed down by gravity. With their boots in the chute, the boys would block pieces of slate, rock, or dirt and pick them out with their hands. New boys in the breaker commonly developed a condition called "red tops," named for the bloodied fingertips that occurred until calluses formed. The work was dusty and dangerous, with boys sometimes falling into the rollers and screens into which the clean coal descended. Separated into various marketable sizes, the coal was loaded into railroad cars at the base of the breaker.

### 15 SINGLE FAMILY DWELLING, c. 1854

Farther west in the village is the first single house, other than the rectory at the eastern end. Houses like this one were occupied by bosses and top miners who had contracts to use crews of men to develop new sections of the mine. In 1856, such houses rented for $3.33 per month.

## PRESBYTERIAN CHURCH SITE, 1859

In November 1857, the Reverend Jonathan Ormond was appointed pastor of Eckley's Presbyterian congregation, which held its gatherings at the village schoolhouse. The partners operating the mine and the town offered to build a single church for both the Presbyterians and Episcopalians to use, but the Presbyterians refused and proceeded to build their own church. The church also housed a school. By the twentieth century, the Protestant population of Eckley was declining greatly; sometime after 1920, the congregation was dissolved and the building removed.

## ST. JAMES EPISCOPAL CHURCH, 1859

Two of Eckley's founding partners, Richard Sharpe and Francis Weiss, established St. James Episcopal Church. The Reverend Peter Russell, husband of Sharpe's sister Sarah, came to the village in 1856 and lived there for a number of years. He also ministered to congregations in White Haven and Hazleton in addition to Eckley, where construction began on St. James Church in 1859, resulting in its consecration early in 1860. The church also had a school.

Like the Presbyterian church, St. James faced a decline in Protestant population in the twentieth century. The building was deconsecrated and then removed in 1938. The structure now on this site is St. Paul's Episcopal Church from White Haven, donated to the state by its congregation for Eckley Miners' Village. One of its windows was dedicated to the man who served as its rector as well as the rector of St. James, Peter Russell.

### 18 FOUNDATION OF ECKLEY HOTEL, c. 1857

The hotel served a range of purposes. The town's only barroom was located there in Eckley's early decades, and the hotel also provided temporary housing for new employees and space for various celebrations and gatherings. When the Coxe family took control of the town and mines after 1885, they stopped the sale of liquor there. In its later years, before it burned in 1925, the hotel served entirely as a boardinghouse.

### 19 DOCTOR'S OFFICE, c. 1855

In Eckley's early decades, the company deducted an amount from each worker's pay for the doctor, who was available to treat illnesses and injuries from accidents in and around the mine. While it was difficult to procure a doctor for a company town under any other arrangement, the company doctor often was viewed as more concerned with the company's interests than the mine workers'. Dr. John S. Wentz served as company doctor for a time and also managed the mine at Eckley for his father-in-law, John Leisenring. At some point early in the 1900s, a nurse resided in the village instead of a doctor. The office is restored to the way it looked in the 1870s and includes an exhibit on the history of the practice of medicine in Eckley and company towns like it.

### 20 SITE OF COMPANY STORE, c. 1855

Like many facets of life in the company town, the company store began because mine workers needed such a facility, but it aroused suspicion because of the monopoly it had. The store sold a wide range of goods, from mining tools and supplies to food, clothes, and housewares. Always controversial was the question of whether prices at the company store were so high as to exploit the workers, whose bills in the early decades were deducted directly from their pay before they received it. This could result in that most hated outcome for workers—receiving nothing on payday, with a "snake" or line at the bottom of the pay notice indicating that there was nothing left after the deduction for the store bill. In contrast to a number of other mine operators who ran company towns, however, Eckley B. Coxe disliked this practice of deducting store bills. He ended it soon after he took control of Eckley at the end of 1885, and by 1900 his company had sold the store. Aside from its utilitarian function, the company store served as a gathering place for Eckley residents, especially since it also housed the town's post office.

## MINE OWNER'S HOUSE, c. 1861

At the far western end of town is Richard Sharpe's house, which is in the process of being restored inside and out to its once grand appearance. All four of the founding partners lived in Eckley for a number of years. Sharpe spent twenty years here, from 1854 to 1874. This Gothic Revival house was the largest of the partners' homes, with fourteen rooms for Sharpe's family of eight and their servants. At that time, a stable and gardens, kept by a full-time gardener, could be found nearby.

## MULE BARN

Mules played a major transportation role in and around anthracite coal mines well into the twentieth century. Although mules were stabled underground at some mines, at Eckley they were taken down into the mine each morning and brought back to the surface each evening. This barn was reconstructed in 1988 from the plans for the original barn. It is close to the original location, which was where the highway is now, a bit farther away from the Mine Owner's House.

## FEED BARN

The feed barn has also been carefully reconstructed according to the original plans. Its reconstruction was completed in 1996.

For more information on hours, tours, programs, and activities at Eckley Miners' Village, visit **www.phmc.state.pa.us** or call **570-636-2070**.

# *Further Reading*

Aurand, Harold W. *From the Molly Maguires to the United Mine Workers:The Social Ecology of an Industrial Union, 1869–1897.* Philadelphia: Temple University Press, 1971.

Bartoletti, Susan Campbell. *Growing Up in Coal Country.* New York: Houghton Mifflin Co., 1999.

Blatz, Perry K. *Democratic Miners: Work and Labor Relations in the Anthracite Coal Industry, 1875–1925.* Albany, N.Y.: State University of New York Press, 1994.

Broehl, Wayne G., Jr. *The Molly Maguires.* New York: Vintage/Chelsea House, 1964.

Dublin, Thomas and George Harvan. *When the Mines Closed: Stories of Struggles in Hard Times.* New York: Cornell University Press, 1998.

Kenny, Kevin. *Making Sense of the Molly Maguires.* New York: Oxford University Press, 1998.

Korson, George. *Minstrels of the Mine Patch: Songs and Stories of the Anthracite Industry.* Philadelphia: University of Pennsylvania Press, 1938.

Landis, Mary Ann. "The 'Struggle' for Ascendancy: The Changing Relationship of the Anthracite Mine Operators and Mine Workers of Pennsylvania's Council Ridge Colliery, 1854–1874." Master's thesis, University of Delaware, 1997.

Noon, Mark. "Martin Ritt Takes on the Molly Maguires." *Pennsylvania Heritage* 27 (fall 2001): 12–21.

Roberts, Peter. *The Anthracite Coal Communities.* New York: Macmillan Co., 1901.

———. *The Anthracite Coal Industry.* New York: Macmillan Co., 1904.

Sharpless, Richard E. and Donald L. Miller. *The Kingdom of Coal: Work, Enterprise, and Ethnic Communities in the Mine Fields.* Philadelphia: University of Pennsylvania Press, 1985.

Warfel, Stephen G. *"A Patch of Land Owned by the Company": Historical and Archaeological Investigations of House Lots #117/119 Main Street, Eckley Miners' Village.* Harrisburg, Pa.: Pennsylvania Historical and Museum Commission, 1993.

Yearley, C. K., Jr. *Enterprise and Anthracite: Economics and Democracy in Schuylkill County, 1820–1875.* Baltimore: Johns Hopkins University Press, 1961.

## Also Available

**Anthracite Heritage Museum and Scranton Iron Furnaces**

**Brandywine Battlefield Park**

**Conrad Weiser Homestead**

**Cornwall Iron Furnace**

**Daniel Boone Homestead**

**Drake Well Museum and Park**

**Ephrata Cloister**

**Erie Maritime Museum and U.S. Brig Niagara**

**Hope Lodge and Mather Mill**

**Joseph Priestley House**

**Landis Valley Museum**

**Old Economy Village**

**Pennsbury Manor**

**Railroad Museum of Pennsylvania**

*All titles are $10, plus shipping, from Stackpole Books, 800-732-3669, www.stackpolebooks.com, or The Pennsylvania Historical and Museum Commission, 800-747-7790, www.phmc.state.pa.us*